BRANCH LINES OF
WEST LONDON

Vic Mitchell and Keith Smith

MP Middleton Press

This album is dedicated to all those who have so willingly and enthusiastically contributed to Middleton Press publications - this is our 250th!

Published August 2000

ISBN 1 901706 50 8

© Middleton Press, 2000

Design Deborah Esher
Typesetting Barbara Mitchell

Published by
> *Middleton Press*
> *Easebourne Lane*
> *Midhurst, West Sussex*
> *GU29 9AZ*
Tel: 01730 813169
Fax: 01730 812601

Printed & bound by Biddles Ltd,
> *Guildford and Kings Lynn*

CONTENTS

INDEX

ACKNOWLEDGEMENTS

We are very grateful for the help received from so many of the photographers. Our thanks also go to G.Croughton, N.Langridge, B.W.Leslie, Mr D. and Dr S.Salter, E.Wilmshurst, E.Youldon and as always, our wives.

I. The GWR branches featured in this album are shown with the stations as existing in the 1930s. (J.C.Gillham)

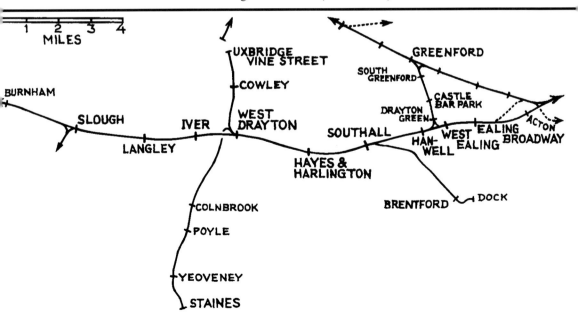

GEOGRAPHICAL SETTING

When constructed all the lines (apart from about two miles of the Staines branch) were in the county of Middlesex, the Brentford branch reaching its county town. The surviving parts have been in Greater London since 1974, except the two miles already mentioned.

All four routes are closely associated with northern tributaries of the River Thames. The Greenford Loop crosses the River Brent, while the Brentford branch is close to it at its southern end. The Uxbridge and Staines lines are in close proximity to the River Colne, the Colne Brook and the Wyrardisbury (now Wraysbury) River, which are roughly parallel to one another north of Staines.

The tracks were laid mostly on Alluvium or Gravels of no revenue benefit to the railways.

The maps are to the scale of 25ins to 1 mile (unless otherwise stated) and have north at the top

HISTORICAL BACKGROUND

The Great Western Railway's main line between Paddington and Maidenhead opened on 4th June 1838, but neither terminus was on the site of the present station. Branches developed from it as described below. The 1998 branch to Heathrow, however, is included in our *Ealing to Slough* album.

Greenford Loop

The route between West Ealing and Greenford (East Junction) was brought into use on 1st July 1904, services to Greenford itself not commencing until 1st October of that year. This station opened that day and was on the new and then incomplete GWR direct route to Birmingham from a junction east of Acton, near Old Oak Common. The first part opened to Park Royal in 1903 and trains reached High Wycombe in 1906. Thus the first trains worked out from, and back to, Paddington via the Loop. The route has always had double track. (An opening date of 3rd June 1903 is sometimes quoted, but this was for a brief usage in connection with an agricultural show.)

Loop line running had been of benefit to the railways operating in the suburbs south of the Thames. This was the GWR's only successful loop; an attempt to create one at Uxbridge failed. The Greenford Loop ran through a thinly populated area, but this had good prospects of housing development.

Brentford Branch

Most of the early railways had to link with the existing waterborne transport system and the GWR had done this by building a canal wharf near Hayes. This had limitations and so an independent company promoted a branch direct to the Thames. It obtained an Act on 14th August 1855 for the Great Western & Brentford Railway, which included provisions for the construction of a dock on the River Thames, an important commercial artery at that time. The branch passed over the London & South Western Railway's 1853 line and opened on 18th July 1859 for goods and on 1st May 1860 for passengers. The single line was laid to broad gauge and a parallel mixed gauge track was brought into use on 1st October 1861. They were worked as single lines, the original one being used for passengers and was soon converted to mixed gauge. Broad gauge was abandoned in June 1875 and the branch became GWR property in 1872. It was double track from 1876.

Passenger services were withdrawn on 22nd March 1915, as a wartime economy measure and reinstated, only after local complaints, on 12th April 1920. Reversion to operation as two single lines occurred on 5th September 1917.

Passenger trains were subsequently lightly used and were withdrawn on 4th May 1942. The branch was singled on 18th December 1955. General goods traffic ceased on 31st December 1964, but part of the branch was retained, as described later.

Staines Branch

The LSWR had started operating to Staines in 1848 and so the enthusiasm for another line was not great. After several Acts, one was passed on 2nd August 1883 which allowed the GWR to build a branch to an independent terminus in the town. The line was opened south to Colnbrook on 9th August 1884 and on to Staines on 2nd November 1885.

The track was never doubled, but a connection (described later) was made to the Southern Railway during World War II. Diesel railcars were introduced in September 1952 on some journeys but full dieselisation did not occur until October 1958. Passenger services were withdrawn on 29th March 1965.

There were no freight trains between Colnbrook and Staines from 1953 to 1964, when an oil terminal was opened at the latter place. The ne south of the former was obliterated by the M25 1981, but reconnection to Southern tracks was made at the southern end for oil trains, which ran until 1991. The route north of Colnbrook was retained to serve private sidings.

Uxbridge Branch

A third and successful Act for the construction of the line was obtained by the GWR in 1853. It was laid to broad gauge and opened on 8th September 1856. Conversion to standard gauge was undertaken on 7-8th October 1871 and doubling followed in 1880.

The branch lost its monopoly on 1st June 1904, when LUT electric trams began to run to Shepherds Bush. The Metropolitan Railway arrived on 4th July 1904 and the GWR's own branch from the north, at Denham, came into use on 1st May 1907.

Partial dieselisation took place in September 1958 but, despite such economy of operation, passenger service withdrawal followed on 10th September 1962. The line was singled on 18th October following and goods traffic continued until 13th July 1964. The southern half mile, to a private siding, was in use from 1966 to 1979.

PASSENGER SERVICES

The figures quoted are for down trains running on at least five days per week.

Greenford Loop

The first timetables gave diverse travel opportunities on the route. There were eight "Motor Cars" from Park Royal to Acton initially, but by 1907 there was one train to Oxford, one to Aylesbury and three to Uxbridge (High Street) from Paddington. There were also seven railmotors running between Westbourne Park and Acton, reversing at Greenford. There were four trips from Greenford to Southall and seven from Willesden Junction to Greenford via Ealing. On Sundays there were twelve trains from Clapham Junction to Greenford via Ealing, plus one from Victoria.

By 1920 there were eleven trains to Greenford via the Loop, mostly originating at Paddington. In 1930, there were five to Greenford, eight to Northolt, seventeen to Ruislip and four to Denham, mostly originating at Paddington. From 1934 to May 1988, most trains started from Ealing Broadway, but reverted to Paddington thereafter. Trains did not run west of Greenford after 20th November 1948.

The service interval has been mostly half-hourly in recent decades.

Brentford Branch

Ten trains were provided initially, this rising to 13 by 1875 and falling to nine by 1902. A daily half-hourly service came with the introduction of railmotors on 2nd May 1904. (They were hourly on Sunday mornings.) After restoration in 1920, they ran on weekdays only, but with a gap between 11.15am and 2.15pm. Sunday trains were tried again in 1923 only. From 1929, a service was provided in peak hours only and was pruned further in 1941 to give just six trips in the mornings and five in the evenings in the final months.

Staines Branch

The 1885 timetable showed trains from West Drayton arriving at the Colnbrook terminus at 9.13am, 2.58pm (from Moorgate Street) and 8.23pm. There were none on Sundays.

The initial service to Staines was one of nine trains, weekdays only. By the end of the century, it had increased to 12. The 1910 timetable showed 15 weekday trains, with nine on Sundays. Some peak hour services originated at Paddington and there were one or two from Aldgate and also Victoria in the 1904-11 period.

From 1914 to 1958 there were about 14 trains daily. With the introduction of a full diesel service in 1958, the timetable was revised to give 18 weekday and 16 Sunday trains. The latter were withdrawn in September 1961. There were 13 trips shown in the final timetable.

Uxbridge Branch

The first timetable showed 15 trains on weekdays and 10 on Sundays. (A through train from Paddington was introduced in 1876). These figures had increased to 45 and 16 by 1913, the former including 14 trains through from London (ten from Paddington, three from Liverpool Street and one from Victoria). By 1938, the branch figures were 46 and 26, but there were only two from Liverpool Street and none from Victoria. The former were withdrawn with the advent of World War II.

There were 35 trains in the 1944 timetable (23 on Sundays), a frequency that was maintained until 1953. Some of these originated at Paddington in peak hours. After 1956, trains ran during weekday peak hours and evenings only. Despite this, the final timetable showed 23 trains.

1. Greenford Loop
WEST EALING

II.   The two mile long line ends at triangular junctions; Greenford is to the left of the top one and West Ealing is to the right of the lower one. The 1945 map is to the scale of 2ins to 1 mile.

(lower left)

1.   The four tracks of the Paddington to Slough main line are in the foreground as no. 1456 takes to the branch with the "Greenford Motor" on 7th August 1955. Milk tankers stand at the depot on the right. Beyond the right edge of the picture is the station, which opened on 1st March 1871 as "Castle Hill". It was "Castle Hill & Ealing Dean" from June 1875 until July 1899, before becoming West Ealing. (R.C.Riley)

2.   Another member of the 1400 class was working on the Greenford Loop on 14th June 1958. No. 1446 is departing, bound for Ealing Broadway. While the station was still gaslit, electric signalling had been introduced in 1955. (H.C.Casserley)

3.   No. 1426 proceeds towards Greenford on 23rd August 1958 and passes platform 4. The other three were west of the bridge from which this photograph was taken. The wide separation of the original tracks on the right was due to them being broad gauge, until 1892. (J.C.Gillham)

4.   Two days after the previous picture had been taken, DMUs were working the Greenford services. On the right is the original goods yard, which was in use until the mid-1960s. The larger yard is shown on the next map. (J.C.Gillham)

5.   No. 6125 is leaving the milk depot with tankers destined for Kensington Olympia via the Greenford Loop on 1st December 1962. Milk traffic ceased around 1978. The siding to the left of the locomotive served Pressings & Stampings Ltd until 1966. The signal box had a new 71-lever frame fitted in 1955 and was in use until 18th March 1968. (T.Heavyside)

6.   Looking north-west from the same view point on 3rd July 1990, we see no. 59005 *Kenneth J. Painter* leaving the Greenford Loop with empty stone wagons from Park Royal, bound for Acton Yard. The eighth wagon is on the level crossing on the road serving the works of Plasser & Theurer, manufacturers of track maintenance equipment. (G.Gillham)

7.   HSTs on the Euston-Holyhead service have to travel empty via the Greenford Loop to reach Old Oak Common Depot for servicing. We witness no. 43030 returning to Euston on 15th September 1993. Platform 1 had been removed in 1973 and platform 4 had been moved west of the road bridge in 1991, hence the row of lights near the rear of the train. The new station building (on the bridge) was opened in 1987. (M.Turvey)

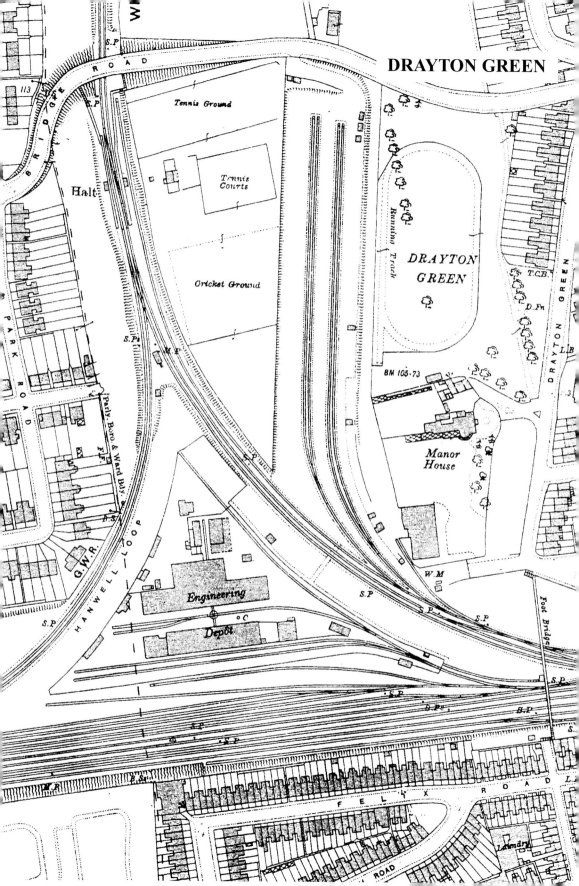

DRAYTON GREEN

8.   This was the second halt to open on the Loop, coming into use on 1st March 1905. A southward view from Drayton Bridge Road in about 1939 includes the footpaths to both platforms, the long siding of West Ealing New Yard and the 23-lever Drayton Green signal box, which closed on 20th March 1955. (Stations UK)

III.   The halt is top left on this 1937 survey and the bridge from which photos 1 and 4 to 7 were taken is lower right. The goods yard was opened in 1908 and the weighing machine (W.M.) had an office adjacent, which can be seen behind the locomotive in picture no. 6. The Hanwell Loop (left) opened on 1st May 1904 and carried a limited number of passenger trains in the early years. It was singled in 1974 at its south end. Goods facilities were withdrawn on 23rd May 1980.

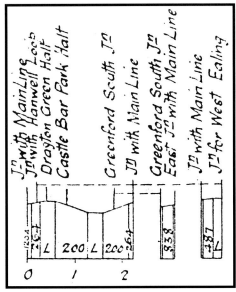

9.   A crossover had been situated behind the railcar until October 1967 and the platforms were subsequently rebuilt slightly closer to the road bridge. The junction was recorded on 12th August 1983, as no. L122 was about to stop by the styleless shelter. (T.Wright)

10.   Passenger comfort was improved with the introduction of the class 165 Thames Turbos on Paddington services in 1992. This example was photographed on 17th September 1996, close to the mirror required for one person operation. There is no evidence that more than two tracks ever passed under the long bridge span. (F.Hornby)

CASTLE BAR PARK

11.   This was the only one of the three halts to open with the line, but it was not close to any dwellings. The term "halt" was dropped in May 1969. The platforms were replaced by concrete ones north of the footbridge in November 1960. This northward view is from the 1950s; in the distance the line passes over the River Brent on a 108yd long viaduct. (R.S.Carpenter coll.)

12.   The 20 mph restriction sign was due to the long-term embankment stability problem between here and South Greenford. This 1963 northward view includes the small ticket office. To the south is the covered way known as Drayton Green Tunnel. It was completed in April 1974 to allow building development and is 506yds in length. (Stations UK)

SOUTH GREENFORD

13.   The halt opened on 20th September 1926, the platforms having previously seen service at Trumpers Crossing, on the Brentford Branch. Seen in 1958, the bridge in the distance was over the A403, now the A40. (Stations UK)

14.   Class 165 Turbo units began working the branch on 11th October 1993 and no. 165132 creeps south on 27th forming the 12.54 from Greenford to Paddington. There was a severe speed restriction and the up platform had been removed during embankment stabilising work. London-bound passengers had to travel via Greenford until 26th October 1999. In the distance is the facing crossover and signals of Greenford South Junction. (M.Turvey)

GREENFORD

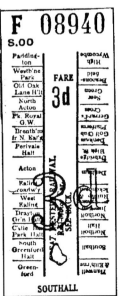

15.   This westward panorama features the GWR main line to Birmingham, which is flanked by the two platform loop lines. Vans largely obscure the goods shed, which was added in 1932, along with two more sidings in the goods yard. This was in use until 23rd May 1980. The LT Central Line tracks were laid behind the left fence. West Box is in the distance; it closed on 8th August 1971, but East Box was still in use in 2000. (LGRP/NRM)

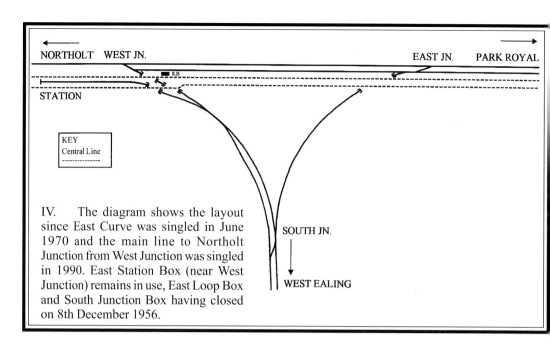

NORTHOLT   WEST JN.   EAST JN.   PARK ROYAL

S.B

STATION

KEY
Central Line
- - - - - - - - - - - - -

SOUTH JN.

↓

WEST EALING

IV.   The diagram shows the layout since East Curve was singled in June 1970 and the main line to Northolt Junction from West Junction was singled in 1990. East Station Box (near West Junction) remains in use, East Loop Box and South Junction Box having closed on 8th December 1956.

16.   A new station was provided for Central Line trains, it opening on 30th June 1947. Services were extended to West Ruislip on 21st November 1948. The station which included this bay for Ealing trains, was built by the GWR and transferred to LT on 1st January 1948. The 0-4-2T and the main line down signals were photographed on 10th November 1957. (A.E.Bennett)

17.   No. 55030 has just passed under the westbound Central Line as it approaches the bay on 13th March 1982. Also evident are the bridges carrying eastbound LT trains over West Curve. The signal is for starting trains from the bay. (A.Dasi-Sutton)

18.   The original platforms were closed on 17th June 1963, although part of the up one can be seen in the background of this photograph from 11th March 1989. The route was down-graded steadily, there being only one passenger train each way by 2000, Monday to Fridays only. A "Bubblecar" waits to leave for Paddington at 15.42 on 11th March 1989. The entrance building was extensively rebuilt in 1993. (P.G.Barnes)

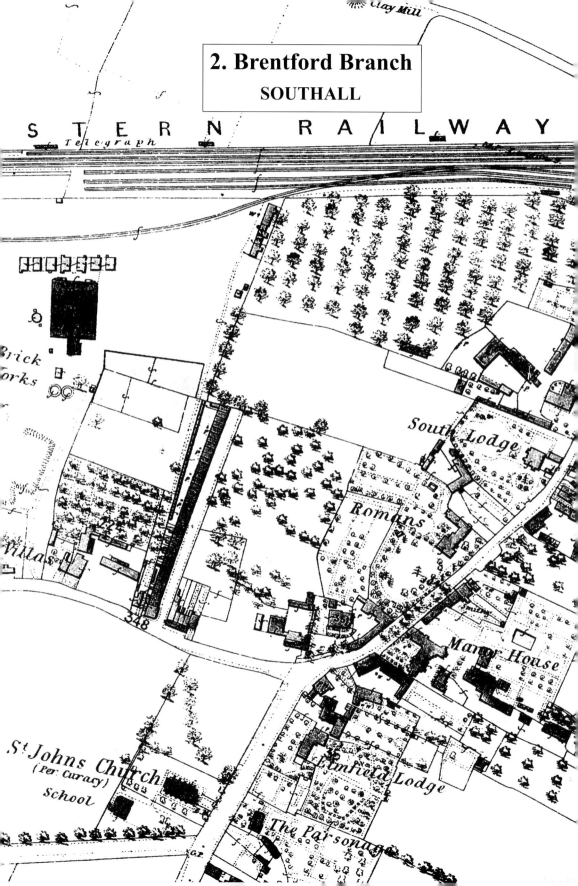

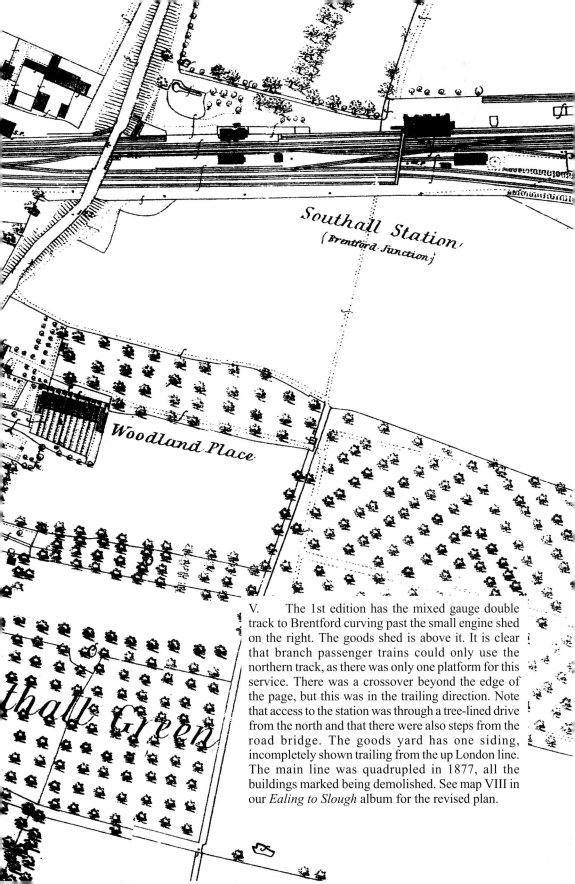

Southall Station
(Brentford Junction)

Woodland Place

thall Green

V.　　The 1st edition has the mixed gauge double track to Brentford curving past the small engine shed on the right. The goods shed is above it. It is clear that branch passenger trains could only use the northern track, as there was only one platform for this service. There was a crossover beyond the edge of the page, but this was in the trailing direction. Note that access to the station was through a tree-lined drive from the north and that there were also steps from the road bridge. The goods yard has one siding, incompletely shown trailing from the up London line. The main line was quadrupled in 1877, all the buildings marked being demolished. See map VIII in our *Ealing to Slough* album for the revised plan.

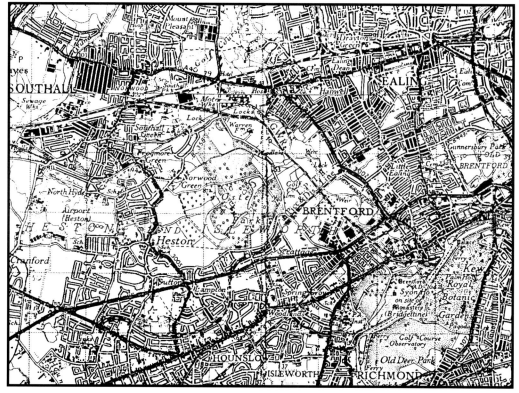

VI.   The 1945 map at 1 ins to 1 mile includes the town, (north of the station), the AEC commercial vehicle works (east of the divergence of the tracks), Heston Airport (left) and Kew Gardens (lower right). It had been intended to convey excursionists thereto via Brentford Dock and a ferry, but the station was not completed.

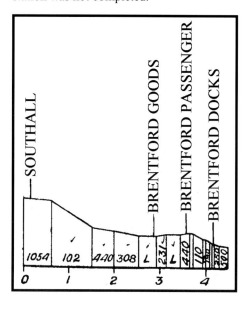

VII.   Gradient profile includes the mileage from the junction west of Southall road bridge.

19.   The 1877 buildings are in the background, the main lines are centre and a train stands on the down relief line to the right. A coach is in the up bay on the far right. Featured in this 1934 westward view is railmotor no. 98, which is smoking while being shunted by a pannier tank. Beyond the latter, a Brentford train waits at the platform. There were 100 such self-propelled cars back in 1913. Introduced to the branch in 1904, they sometimes had to haul a coach at busy times. (B.Y.Williams)

20.   Turning round at exactly the same viewpoint, we see the Brentford lines curving to the right of the 1884 engine shed. Beyond the telegraph pole is the coal stage and to the right of it is the 1905 water softener tower, behind which is the water tank. A margarine factory is on the right of this 1919 panorama. (R.M.Casserley coll.)

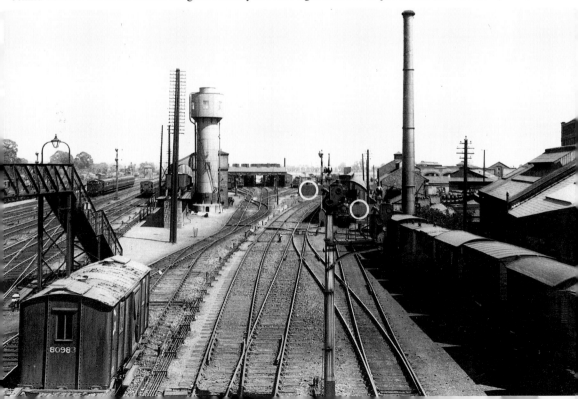

21.   No. 3596 is near the end of the Brentford platform and close to the public footbridge from which pictures 19, 20, 22, 24, 25 and 26 were taken. The span for staff, seen in the previous picture, links to it. The 3500 "Metro" class was introduced by Dean in 1899 for local traffic and a few survived to become BR property. (J.G.Sturt)

22.   Seen on 10th August 1957 is 0-4-2T no. 1406 standing outside the shed, which was erected in 1904 to house the branch railmotor. Since the singling in 1955, the line adjacent to the shed ran only to the Quaker Oats premises, visible in the right background. The AEC siding branches left from the running line in the distance. (R.C.Riley)

23.   An up train from Brentford is hauled by no. 9726 on 15th May 1963 and passes the signal seen in the previous picture. It is signalled for the goods line through the station. There were usually seven freight trains each way on weekdays in the 1930s. (P.Hay)

24.   No. 47077 leaves West Yard on 9th June 1978 with rubbish containers destined for Brentford. The roadside building had been halved in length (see no. 19), but the mighty gas holder and castellated water tower were still standing. East Box had stood just beyond the right border of the picture until 1968. (T.Heavyside)

25.   The engine shed seen in picture 20 was enlarged to eight roads in 1954 and was used for steam locos and a few diesel railcars until the end of 1965. It subsequently accommodated DMUs until November 1986. An enthusiasts special is leaving the branch in September 1981. (R.Palmer)

26.　　Another special was recorded on 22nd June 1991, this time headed by nos 37682 and 37685. The "Brentford Bard" was its name; the subtitle was "A mid-summers night dream". All trains for the branch had to reverse in West Yard until March 1995. (P.G.Barnes)

27.　　The goods yard, north of the main line, closed in 1967 and its goods shed was later leased by the GWR Preservation Group for rolling stock restoration. It moved to the shed seen in picture 25 in 1988. The 1948 RSH 0-4-0ST *Birkenhead* and ex-GWR 2-8-0 no. 2885 were recorded on 15th May 1996. The group's lease was terminated in favour of Flying Scotsman Railway in July 1997, but its stock remained in a nearby siding for several years, pending a new home. (M.Turvey)

SOUTH OF SOUTHALL

28.   Viewed from the first bridge on the branch on 24th May 1987 is no. 56033, approaching
Southall with loaded rubbish containers. Like the "night soilmen" of old, this is normally a nocturnal
activity, but it was possible to photograph the train early on Sunday mornings. This is the 08.50 from
Brentford to Appleford, which is north of Didcot. (B.Morrison)

29.   One mile from the station, we come to "Three Bridges", so called because the canal and a road cross railway arches at the same point. A horse and well loaded cart are on Windmill Lane, while two other horses tow a barge on the Grand Junction (later Grand Union) Canal. The lower arches act as buttresses. (J.E.Connor coll.)

30.   Passing the extensive AEC Works on 13th September 1960 is 0-6-0PT no. 3620, bound for Brentford. Figures for the branch for the year of 1956 showed 218,409 tons of general merchandise conveyed. This excluded coal and other minerals. (T.Wright)

31.   A westward view from Windmill Lane in 1968
includes an RCTS special train and the AEC Works
again. The water is probably from the canal aqueduct,
which was constructed from 140 tons of cast iron
forming an 8ft. deep trough. This is one of the last works
for which I.K.Brunel was responsible before his death.
(T.Wright)

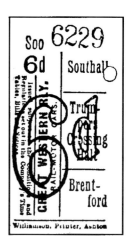

TRUMPERS CROSSING HALT

32.   The platforms were opened on 2nd May 1904 with the introduction of railmotors. However, the train seen here is an autocoach propelled by an encased class 517 0-4-2T, no. 833. Mr. Trumper had been an uncooperative landowner, so it is surprising to find his name on the board; also an E on HALT. This is thought to be due to the railcar concept having come from France. (LPC/NRM)

33.   A southward view about 500 yds from the site of the halt includes the peaceful River Brent, the noisy M4 and the smoky train seen in picture 31. The halt closed for the second time on 1st February 1926 and was rebuilt at South Greenford, as shown in photograph no. 13. (T.Wright)

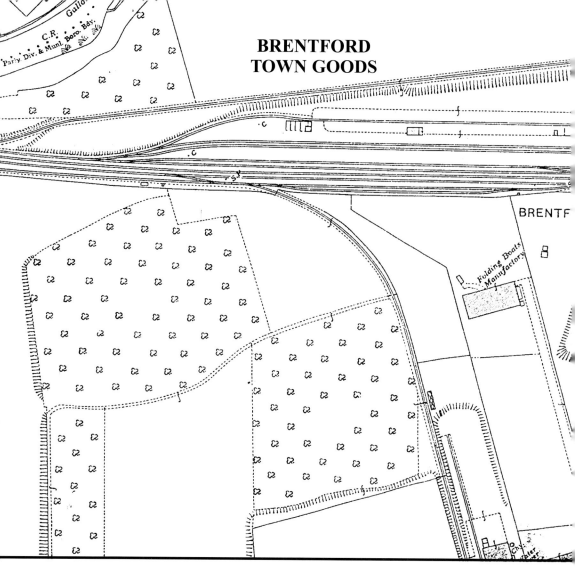

BRENTFORD
TOWN GOODS

BRENTF

Folding Boats Manufactory

VIII.   The construction of the Great West Road (right page) in 1925 gave the opportunity to create a new and easily accessible goods yard. It opened on 3rd November 1930. Private sidings were provided for MacFarlane, Lang & Company's biscuit factory (left page, lower) and the Firestone Tyre & Rubber Company (right page) in 1928. There were two 6-ton cranes and access to the Grand Union Canal. This 1935 map is at the scale of 20 ins to 1 mile. Vertically on the right is the SR Hounslow Loop line.

34.   The access road and goods shed are visible as we look north-west from a point near the Great West Road. The 33-lever Firestone Box was in use until 31st May 1964. (R.C.Riley)

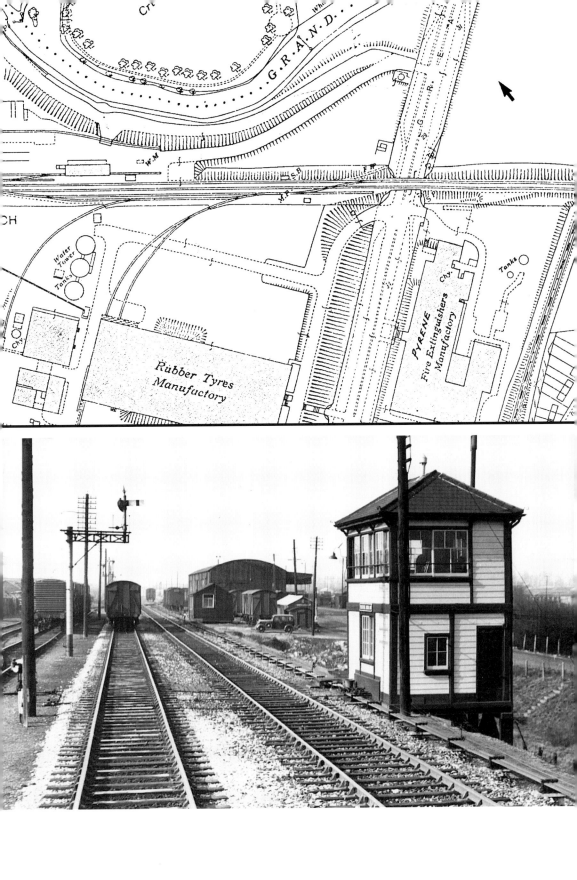

35.　　The Great West Road (A4) acted as a bypass to Brentford and was among the first to be built as a dual carriageway. It thus required an unusually long bridge. A Thames Valley Bristol Lodekka is passing under the impressive structure in April 1961. Demolition took place in March 1976. There was another bridge, to the left, over the Waterloo-Hounslow line of the Southern Region. (J.C.Gillham)

36.　　The Locomotive Club of Great Britain and the Railway Enthusiasts Club ran a railtour jointly on 25th July 1965. It was photographed in bad light from near the site of the signal box. General goods traffic ceased on 7th December 1970. (M.Furnell)

37.　　Private sidings were retained south of the Piccadilly Line bridge, seen here from the south in May 1993. On the right is Day's Siding, used by Aggregate Industries, and in the distance is the loop line and a siding. Limestone came from Croft Quarry in Leicestershire. (J.C.Gillham)

38.　　Looking south from the same railtour, we see the disused siding of Perry Metals and the West London Refuse Transfer Station in the distance. This was created on the site of the goods yard in 1977. A 30-year contract has resulted in six trains per week on the branch. Each has 20 wagons, the total load being about 800 tons. Two trains operate the service. (J.C.Gillham)

BRENTFORD

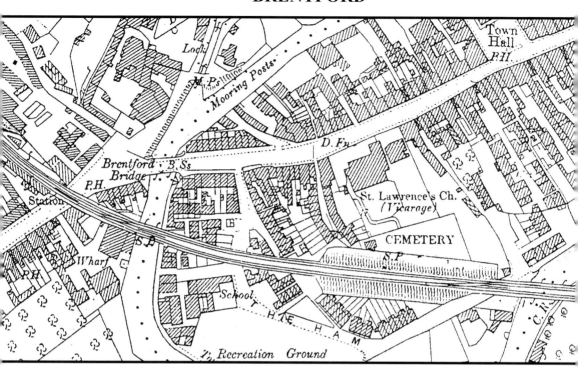

39.   By the time that this view towards the Docks was taken in the 1930s, only the right platform was in use. It seems that the northern one came first and that the other was added for standard gauge trains. Their history is uncertain, but the down platform (left) appears to have been used for arrivals and the up one for departures during the initial period of double track operation. The trailing crossover west of the station was reversed in 1905, the facing arrangement allowing trains to arrive at the up platform. The exit from the down platform was via a ramp and through an arch under the tracks. (Stations UK)

IX.   The 1895 map has the Town Hall and High Street on the right, and the station and canalised River Brent on the left.

40.   An autocoach obscures the locomotive in this close-up of the neglected station in its final days. Beyond the train is a ringed shunt signal controlling movement from the Docks. (Lens of Sutton)

41.   A 12-lever box had been situated on the down platform from 1876 to 1904. Its successor is shown here and can be seen in the background of the previous two pictures. It had 19 levers and was in use until 31st January 1954, leaving Firestone as the only box on the branch. The High Street bridge is also evident. (Lens of Sutton)

42.   The RCTS "West London Rail Tour" on 13th October 1956 gave many their last opportunity to see the station, as it was demolished in the following year. Ex-LMS 2-6-4T no. 42595 proceeds to the Docks crossover. The last regular passenger train had been on 3rd May 1942. (T.Wright)

43.   An October 1958 photograph reveals the unimposing entrance and also the signal box base. Internal stairs gave access to the platform. Electric trams were introduced here in 1901, the later 1906 Hanwell route competing with the GWR branch. The embankment west of the station is illustrated in picture 62 in the Middleton Press *Hammersmith and Hounslow Tramways*. Trolleybuses ran here from 1935 to 1962. (J.C.Gillham)

BRENTFORD DOCK

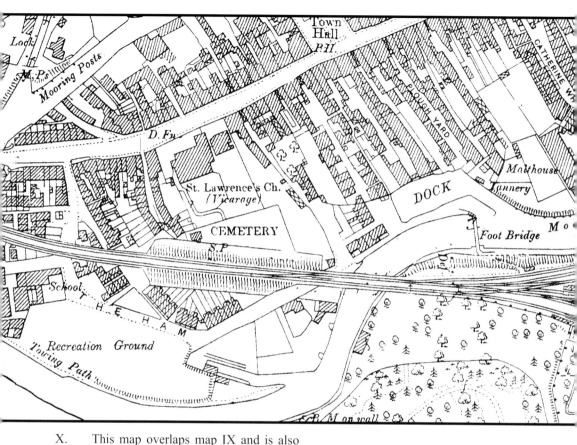

X.   This map overlaps map IX and is also from 1895. On the right page is the lock and sluice at the end of the River Brent and also the gate to Brentford Dock from the River Thames. The goods shed (near the left of the right page) spans water and two sidings. There were eleven hydraulic hoists therein. The unused platform for the Kew Gardens traffic was reported as near the other shed, which was used for local traffic.

44.   Nos. 3619 and 7730 stand on parallel tracks above The Ham (see left page of the map), near the crossovers, on 10th October 1958. Even after the end of steam, two class 08 diesel shunters were required here. The viaduct east of the station was 233yds in length. (J.C.Gillham)

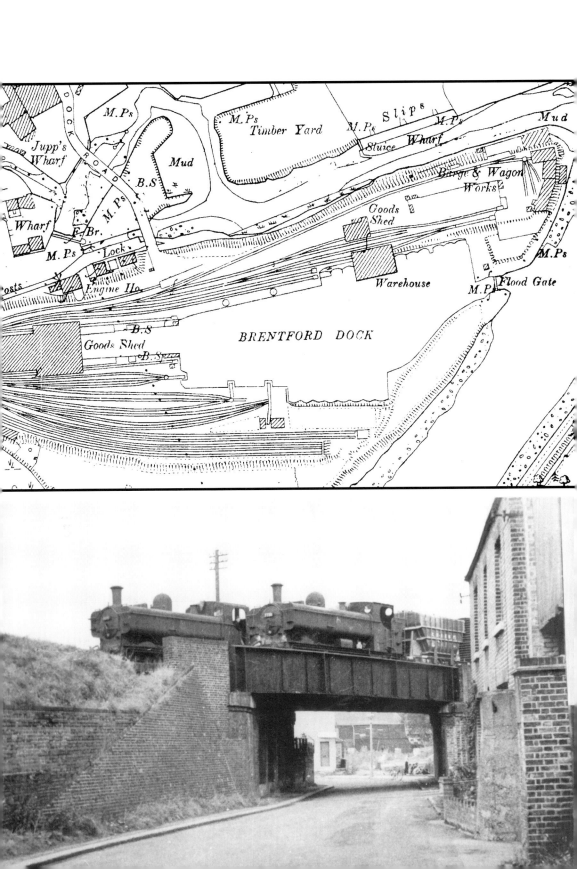

BRENTFORD DOCK

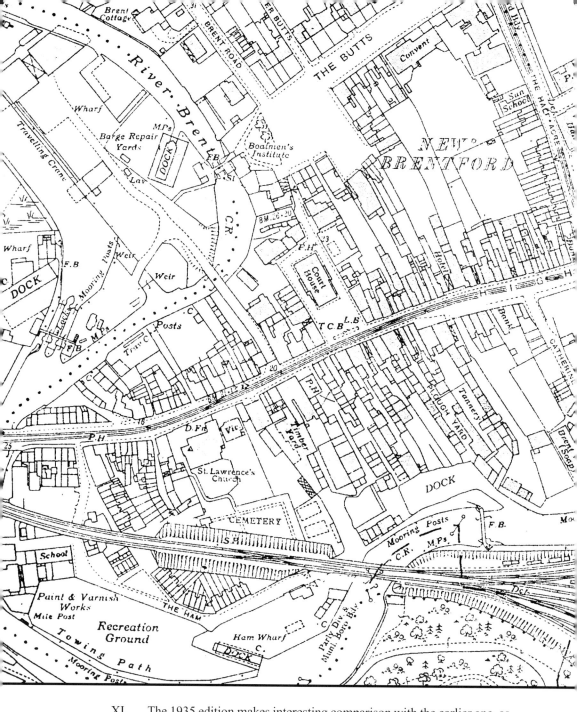

XI.   The 1935 edition makes interesting comparison with the earlier one, as the Thames frontage was changed greatly in 1919, when the area was redeveloped. The transfer shed, which was designed by Brunel, was burnt down in 1920, but rebuilt on the same site and termed the "Shipping Shed". The 29ft gate could accommodate vessels of up to 300 tons. The street tramways are also shown, including the one to Hanwell, the trams on which started in the Half Acre.

Children's Playground

School

Hell

ALEXANDRA ROAD

ST PAUL'S ROAD

Motor Works
Motor Repair
Chy.

TOWN MEADOW RD.

F.E. Sta.

FERRY SQ.

FERRY LANE

Thames Soap Works (Disused)

G.W.M.

Refuse Destructor

Chy.

Corporation Yard

Chy.

M.P

C

Trav. Crane

Co

C

Hay & Straw Depot

Mud

DOCK ROAD

WHARF

Mud

Und.

Mud

Mud

Trav. Crane

Wharf

M.Ps

H.W.M.M.T.

M.Ps

H.W.M.M.T.

Posts

F.B.
M.P C
F.B Posts
Weir
M.Ps
Lock
Eng. House

DOCK

C.C.

M.P

P. Del.

C

C

C

B.S
C
Cn

Mooring Post

Warehouse

Flood Gate

M.Ps

Warehouse

BRENTFORD DOCK

Goods Shed

Wareho.

Warehouse

Bollards

Travelling Cranes

Bollards

B.S

Old England

Bollards

SURREY

45.   A panorama from the west, on 8th March 1958, includes the Shipping Shed and nos. 8750 and 7731 working North and South Yards respectively. A regular traffic in the 1950s had been the export of Morris cars from Oxford. Three electric capstans had been added in 1932 to facilitate shunting. (R.C.Riley)

46.   On the right is one of the 40-ton hydraulic cranes installed in 1919 and alongside is one of two electrically operated travelling cranes supplied in 1932. This 1958 westward view includes the Shipping Shed on the left. Goods landed here included steel, timber, pulp, flour, feedstuffs and cork. Items despatched included various metals, food products and china clay. The area has since been redeveloped as a marina. (R.C.Riley)

47.   Despite the hoists, much manual labour was required in the Shipping Shed and elsewhere. Most of the traffic had to be transhipped again in the London Docks and, with the advent of containerisation, the inevitable closure came on 31st December 1964. There had been coal traffic in both directions and a block train owned by the Brentford Gas Company once conveyed coke daily from its Southall Gas Works for despatch by water. Other aspects of river traffic can be found in the Middleton Press *London to Portsmouth Waterway*. (GWR Magazine)

3. Staines Branch
WEST DRAYTON

XII.   The entire branch is included in this extract from the 1ins to 1 mile 1945 edition. ⟶

XIII.   The gradient profile includes the earlier name for Yeoveney.

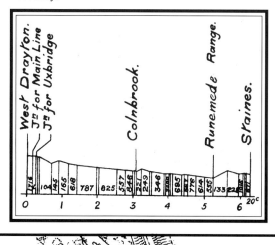

48.   The main lines are in the foreground and East Box is in the distance in this general view from the 1950s. The buildings date from after 1879, when the quadrupling from Slough was completed. The new relief lines were added on the north side, necessitating demolition of the goods shed shown on the map. (Lens of Sutton)

XIV.   The 1st edition was published a few years before the Staines branch opened in 1884. The 2nd edition appears as maps XIII and XIV in our *Ealing to Slough* album. Here we see that the station was originally west of the main road, the bridge over which is to the left of the page join.

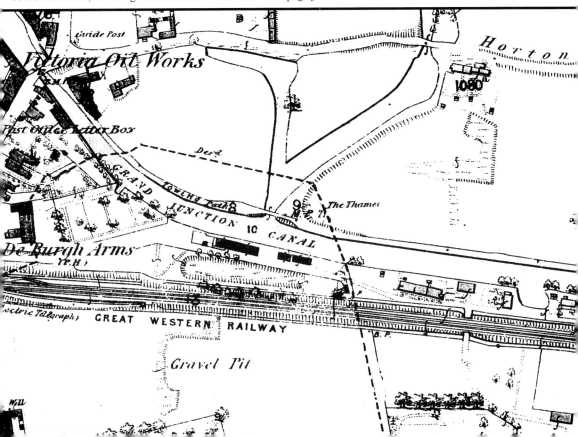

49.   The loop for branch trains was also moved further north. The Staines train is seen at the east end of it on 22nd August 1955, with timber on the canal wharf on the left. (R.M.Casserley)

50.   AEC railcar no. W21W runs onto the up relief line at the east end of the station as it departs empty to its depot at Southall on 27th April 1960. There was a ground frame on the left between 1964 and 1970. There were two sidings in the distance until 1969. (T.Wright)

51.   Four photographs follow that were taken on the last day of services to Staines West, 27th March 1965. The train had just passed West Box, which came into use on 16th May 1960, replacing one that had been south of the main line. (T.Wright)

52.   The Staines train is viewed from the Uxbridge branch. The 66-lever signal box had taken over the functions of East Box on 9th February 1964, but was itself closed on 21st September 1970. There had been double track for 250yds along the Staines curve until 29th May 1927. (T.Wright)

53.   An up train passes under the main line bridge which had been recently rebuilt. On the right is a Coal Dues Obelisk. Tax had been paid on coal entering the Metropolitan area for about six centuries, up to 1890. The track was double the other side of the bridge from 21st July 1940 until 5th September 1952. Loop Signal Box was on the left of the rear coach and was in use between those dates. (T.Wright)

54.   The full name shown on the running-in board was in use from 1895 to 1974. Two identical branch trains standing in the same platform were prone to cause confusion. Your author speaks from experience in the blackout of wartime. (T.Wright)

55.   A coal concentration depot was created in the area enclosed by the loop of the Staines branch. It was officially opened on 18th December 1963 and closed to rail traffic on 7th April 1999. This photograph was taken six months later. It replaced 23 smaller depots and could handle 23 different grades of fuel, mostly coal from the East Midlands and anthracite from South Wales. To the left of the poles is the 1914 up goods line from Iver. (V.Mitchell)

SOUTH OF WEST DRAYTON

56.　　The Thorney Mill sidings are viewed northwards from the first road bridge on the branch, which is ½ mile south of the main line. They came into use on 11th July 1943. The railcar is proceeding north on 12th October 1963. (T.Wright)

57.　　A southward view in 1965 shows more clearly that the northern part of the site was used for scrap metal. This continued until 1989. The road bridge and coal sidings are in the distance. Tonnages for 1975 were: steel 360, stone 3000 and oil 1000, per week on average. (J.C.Gillham)

58.   A firebox is being cut up in front of class 4 2-6-4T no. 80148 on 13th March 1965. The stone terminal has been operated by Aggregate Industries (Bardon) since 1986 and was still in use in 2000. (T.Wright)

59.   No. D4026 runs light past the sidings on 2nd August 1970, as bitumen is being unloaded. This had to be steam heated first, to reduce its viscosity. Subsequently the sidings were used by Mitchell Cotts for oil traffic. The line southwards was disused from January 1981 until May 1990. (T.Wright)

60.   The sidings are in the distance, as a solitary railcar passes through the ruined countryside on a dull and snowy morning in March 1965. The despoilation mattered little, as concrete covered most of the area later, when the massive M4/M25 interchange was built over the line here. (T.Wright)

61.   First was a simple bridge for the M4, built in 1964 and photographed in August 1965. It was to be almost 20 years before the M25 was completed. Between the rails is experimental equipment used for trials on driverless trains. (J.C.Gillham)

COLNBROOK ESTATE HALT

62.   A latecomer to the railway map, the halt was built on the west side of the track and opened on 1st May 1961. The A4, which acted as the Colnbrook Bypass, is in the background in this March 1965 photograph of no. W55022 running north. (T.Wright)

63.   North of the halt, there was a siding on the west side of the line serving Square Grip Reinforcements Ltd. It was laid in 1957, replacing an earlier loop line provided for W.Boyers. No. 4697 is leaving the private siding on the Lakeside Estate on 8th June 1964. (T.Wright)

COLNBROOK

XV.   The dots and dashes on this 1894 map represent the boundary between the southernmost part of Buckinghamshire and the western end of Middlesex. Apart from provision of private sidings, the layout changed little until closure of the goods yard on 3rd January 1966.

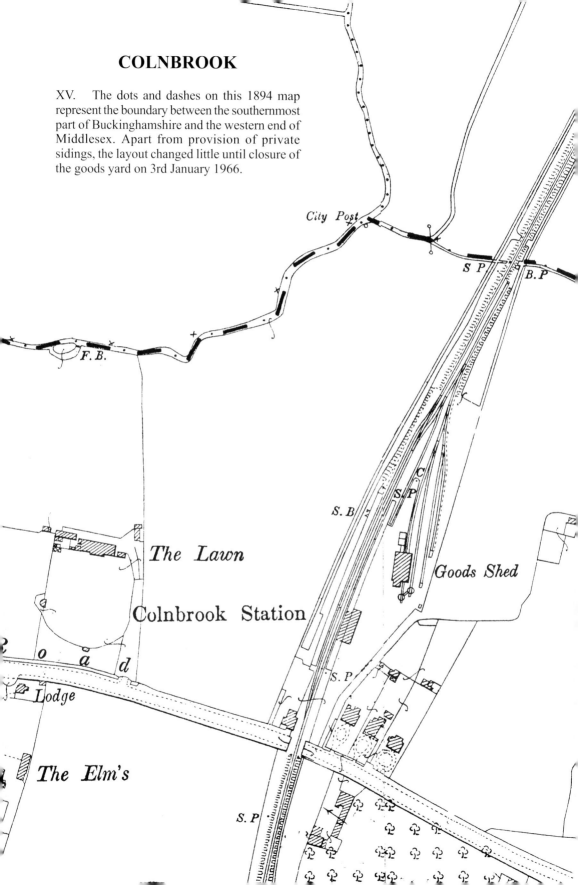

City Post

S P

B. P

F. B.

S. B

C

S. P

The Lawn

Goods Shed

Colnbrook Station

S. P

o   a   d

Lodge

The Elm's

S. P

64.   An early postcard confirms the rural setting of the station, which was nearly one mile east of the village that it served. Its claim to fame was that the Cox's Orange Pippin Apple originated there in 1825. (Lens of Sutton)

65.   The station was a terminus from 9th August 1884 until 2nd November 1885. The up platform (right) was opened on 2nd May 1904, after which time passenger trains could pass here. This is from another undated postcard. (Lens of Sutton)

66. Undated, but from the BR era, this picture shows that some of the lamp glass was opaque. To warn road users of the presence of the crossing, the east and west aspects were red. The gas mantles had been replaced with electric bulbs. (LPC/NRM)

67. With the early style cats whiskers and common exhaust silencer evident, no. W55016 and trailer car were pictured in perfect lighting at 5.20pm on 16th May 1959. Passengers had to use the crossing in the foreground. (J.H.Aston)

68. Less pleasing in appearance, but equally functional, were the Western Region's parcel cars. No. W55992 was recorded bound for Staines on 8th May 1963. Classified 128, some of the fleet of eight were used on the Midland Region. (T.Wright)

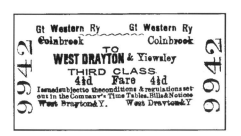

Gt Western Ry   Gt Western Ry
Colnbrook   Colnbrook
            TO
WEST DRAYTON & Yiewsley
        THIRD CLASS
        4½d   Fare   4½d
Issued subject to the conditions & regulations set
out in the Company's Time Tables, Bills & Notices
West Brayton & Y.   West Drayton & Y.

9942   9942

69.   No. W55028 is at the north end of the loop, as it runs towards West Drayton on 10th March 1964. Note that there were two starting signals in close proximity to one another. Diesel units had taken over from steam entirely on 5th October 1958. (T.Wright)

70.   Having completed its shunting at Colnbrook on 8th June 1964, no. 4697 went back over the crossing and is seen proceeding towards West Drayton. Weeds grow on the platform although passenger traffic continued until 27th March of the next year. (T.Wright)

71.   Looking into the light on 29th August 1965, the extent of the yard can be seen. The private siding for Pike Bros is the one on the left. Direct access to the dock road was possible after 1967. (J.C.Gillham)

72.   A panorama in the opposite direction on the same day includes the A4 bridge, Edmund Nuttall's siding branching left near the signal and the yard crane, which was of 6-ton capacity. The siding had come into use in November 1937 and was used in connection with that firm's civil engineering activities. (J.C.Gillham)

73.   The replacement bus service showed all the stations on the blinds. It was being worked by RT1163 on 8th January 1971, a day cold enough to have a cover over half its radiator. There would be no more 6-car DMUs to Paddington, although they had never been advertised as through trains. (T.Wright)

74.   Few signal boxes had such an unusual relationship to crossing gates. The 21-lever frame had been used as a block post until 19th March 1967, after which time it was a ground frame. The date is 7th September 1975. The road had once carried all traffic between London and Bath. (T.Wright)

75.   The sign in the previous picture might seem obvious, but it was ignored by one driver, hence the replacement flags. They are seen on 30th July 1978, the day of the "Farewell Special", which proved not to be the last train. The gate wheel is still evident. (T.Wright)

76.   Regular freight to Staines had ceased on 20th October 1953, but oil trains began to travel there from 24th June 1964, often steam hauled initially. This January 1981 picture includes the flashing lights installed to protect such trains. They ceased to run that year, owing to the branch being severed in favour of the M25.
 (J.C.Gillham)

77.   Seen in September 1993 is the concrete block provided to deter errant drivers proceeding onto the road. Having been disused since 1981, the branch reopened south of Thorney Mill Sidings on 1st March 1990 to bring aviation fuel to the terminal here, which had been established earlier for emergency use. Pipes now convey the fuel to Heathrow Airport and a major new freight interchange facility was announced as this book went to press. (T.Wright)

POYLE ESTATE HALT

78.   Another industrial estate on the branch was served by a halt. This was opened on 4th January 1954 on the west side of the line and was photographed on 1st March 1965. (T.Wright)

POYLE HALT

79.   Opened as Stanwell Moor & Poyle Halt on 1st June 1927, the small wooden structure served a thinly populated area, as reference to map XII will show. Seen in September 1963, the hut was destroyed by fire on 5th October 1964. (T.Wright)

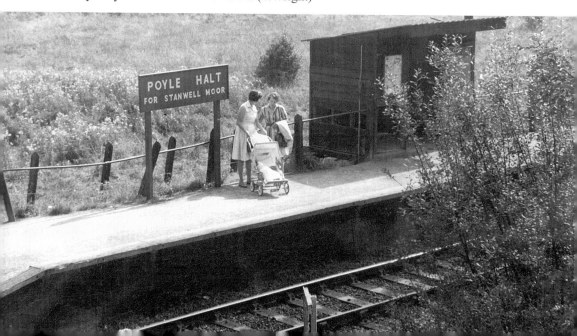

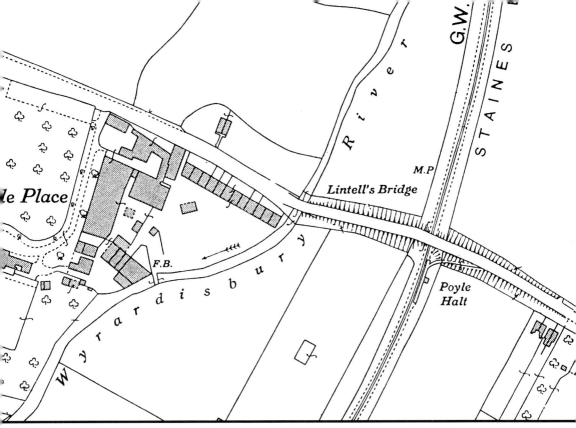

XVI. The 1936 survey indicates some habitation nearby. Lintell's refers to the bridge over the river, not the railway.

80.   Although an unclassified road, the lane had cats eyes, but no footway. Visibility was poor for emerging passengers. The original name was reversed on 26th September 1927, but the term "halt" was retained on this branch until its demise. (T.Wright)

81.   By August 1965, nature was beginning to take over, but the experimental wiring was still in place, although in a different form from that seen elsewhere. (J.C.Gillham)

82.   The new Wraysbury Reservoir is in the background as the track lifting crane stops near the contractor's crossing on 25th March 1981. Junction 14 of the M25 was soon to be built on this site, part of the motorway to Junction 13 being laid over the trackbed. (T.Wright)

STOP
SOUND HORN,
PROCEED WHEN
CROSSING
IS CLEAR.

SHUNT WITH CARE

YEOVENEY

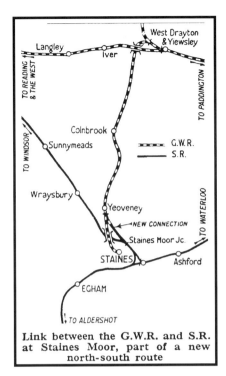

Link between the G.W.R. and S.R. at Staines Moor, part of a new north-south route

XVII. For use in wartime emergencies, a connection was laid between the branch and the Southern Railway. It was usable between 23rd June 1940 and 16th December 1947, but conveyed little traffic. Experience showed that bomb damage to main lines could be repaired within a day or two in most cases. (Railway Magazine)

83.   Looking south from the decaying platform, we see the disused connecton to the SR. Opened as Runemede Range on about 1st April 1887, it served rifle ranges. As some passengers expected to find the Magna Carta here, its name was changed on 4th November 1935. It closed before the other halts, on 14th May 1962. (Lens of Sutton)

84. The Wyrardisbury River is west of the line north of the bridge (right) over the Southern Region Windsor line. Behind the "Bubblecar" on 25th March 1965 is the fixed distant signal for Staines West. (T.Wright)

85. This picture slightly overlaps the previous one and includes the bridge carrying the Windsor line over the river. The arch in the distance carried a farm lane; a similar one was provided over our route. The Staines Bypass (A30) was built this side of them, hence the new concrete span. A short span was provided over the branch. The armless bracket signal was for the wartime spur. (T.Wright)

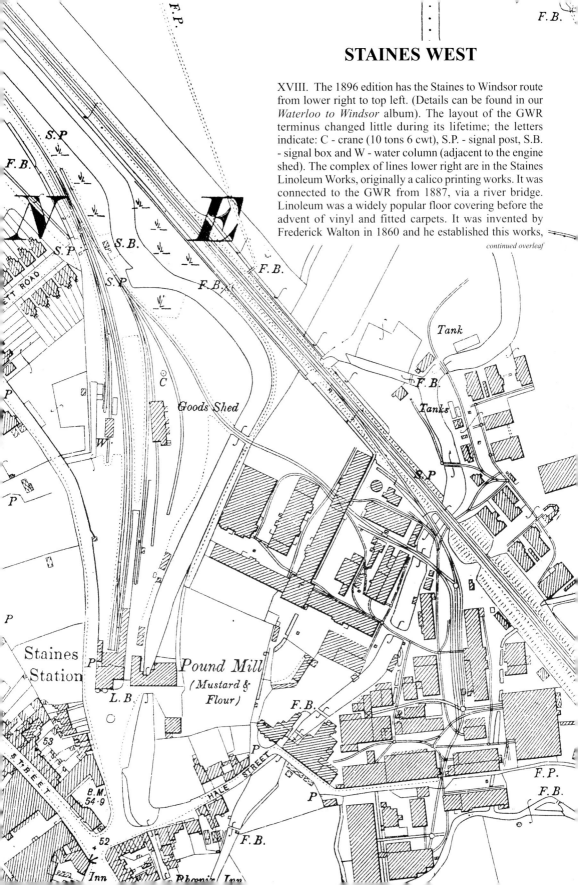

STAINES WEST

XVIII. The 1896 edition has the Staines to Windsor route from lower right to top left. (Details can be found in our *Waterloo to Windsor* album). The layout of the GWR terminus changed little during its lifetime; the letters indicate: C - crane (10 tons 6 cwt), S.P. - signal post, S.B. - signal box and W - water column (adjacent to the engine shed). The complex of lines lower right are in the Staines Linoleum Works, originally a calico printing works. It was connected to the GWR from 1887, via a river bridge. Linoleum was a widely popular floor covering before the advent of vinyl and fitted carpets. It was invented by Frederick Walton in 1860 and he established this works,

continued overleaf

F.P.

F.B.

S.P.

F.B.

S.P.

S.B.

F.B.

F.B.

S.P.

Tank

F.B.

Tanks

C

Goods Shed

S.P.

W.

P

P

Staines
Station

P

L.B.

Pound Mill
*(Mustard &
Flour)*

F.B.

B.M.
54·9

53

STREET

HALE STREET

P

F.B.

P

F.P.

F.B.

52

Inn

Phoenix Inn

the world's first, soon after. Raw materials brought in by rail included linseed oil, resins, cork and pigments, which were mixed and pressed into the oxidised oil on coarse canvas between steam heated rollers, the process requiring large quantities of coal. (Latin: *linum* - linen and *oleum* - oil.)

Below: A northward view from the public footpath (F.P.) includes standard and 3ft 2ins trackwork within Staines Linoleum Works. (Staines Museum)

86.   An Edwardian postcard includes the goods yard entrance, which is behind the non-specific road sign. A red triangle indicated danger, but its nature was not revealed. Passengers would arrive to the gentle sound of water working the mill and the aroma of a generous coating of dung in the street. (Lens of Suttton)

87.   Autocoach no. 117 was an early example, with vertical boards instead of the later steel panels. It has steps that could be swung out to collect passengers where there were no platforms, but they were seldom used. (Lens of Sutton)

88.   The suffix "West" was added by BR on 26th September 1949, somewhat belatedly. Change was often slow: the locomotive is still showing its previous initials 4½ years after nationalisation. This is our only clear view of the goods shed. (R.C.Riley)

89.   The engine shed was photographed on 3rd July 1952; it had officially closed in the previous month, but the rails remained in place until 1964. A pannier tank stands in the goods yard, which closed on 20th October 1953. The track over the river to the lino works was lifted in 1957. (D.B.Clayton)

———————→

90.   Ex-GWR railcar no. W27W departs on 17th March 1956 and we have an opportunity of seeing the signal box, which had 14 levers. It was down graded to a ground frame on 12th July 1959 and closed completely on 20th April 1960. (H.C.Casserley)

———————→

91.   Smartly turned out, nos. W31W and W27W were photographed on 23rd June 1957, when traffic was still reasonably good. They were built in 1940 with 48 seats each and with two 130bhp engines each. The dock in the foreground was little used. (A.E.Bennett)

92.   Passengers defected to private cars as roads improved in the 1960s. A class 121 unit approaches the station on 20th February 1964, having passed under the 1961 bridge under the Staines Bypass. On the right is the Wyrardisbury River and the Windsor line can be seen through its bridge. (T.Wright)

⟶

93.   To save money, an existing private house, built in 1820, was used as the terminal building and the platform was built in its back garden. It had been the home of Charles Finch, owner of the nearby mustard mill. No. W55023 was recorded on 15th March 1964, just over 12 months before passenger services ceased. (T.Wright)

⟶

94.   Shell Mex & BP created a terminal for heating oil on the goods yard site and opened it on 24th June 1964, at a time when central heating was becoming more common. The compound was photographed in 1965, when Cory were undertaking the distribution. (J.C.Gillham)

95. An oil train arrives on 30th July 1965 behind ex-GWR 2-6-2T no. 6134. Steam was used for the first few months only; the trains originated from Ripple Lane, Barking, in Essex. (T.Wright)

96. Upon arrival, the trains ran into the platform and the locomotive ran round the train before propelling it into the siding. Hymek no. D7065 is about to do so on 27th April 1966. (T.Wright)

97. The station approach was the terminus for the LT Central Area routes shown, as well as 203 (Twickenham) and the Kingston buses (216 and 218). The house used for the station was neglected following closure, being empty for eleven years. It was listed in 1976 and is now used as offices. (Lens of Sutton)

98.	Three photographs from 24th January 1981 show the new connection between the Southern and Western Regions; three days later Staines West was officially transferred from the latter to the former. The link had become necessary owing to the need to build the M25 on the route of the southern part of the branch which can be seen on the left and also in the far distance in the form of the bridge shown in picture 85. The line on the right is to Windsor. (J.C.Gillham)

99.	A nine-coach BR special train leaves the Windsor line to cross the new bridge on which men are standing in the previous picture. This was the first train to cross it and the last to run the full length of the branch on its return journey to Paddington. It ran out and back to Windsor & Eton Riverside, via West Drayton and Staines Central, where it reversed. Outwards it used the Greenford Loop. (J.C.Gillham)

100.   The Windsor line is on the left of the river in this southward view. Arriving oil trains had to run north and under the bridge seen in picture 92, before reversing down the line on the right into the depot in the background. There were two to six trains per week, depending on the time of year, but they ceased entirely on 24th June 1991 and all the new work was wasted. (J.C.Gillham)

4. UXBRIDGE BRANCH

XIX. The full length of the 1856 branch is shown on the 1945 map at 1ins to 1 mile. The other two railways to the town are also to be seen.

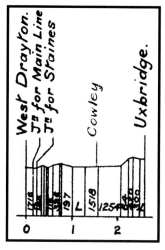

XX. The official gradient profile shows that the branch was 2½ miles in length.

COWLEY

101.   The branch had through trains to Paddington for most of its life. One such was recorded on 20th May 1958, behind 2-6-2T no. 6161. At that time there were departures on weekday mornings at 6.13, 8.3, 8.21 and 8.58 and they included first class accommodation. (T.Wright)

102.   Viewed on the same day as no. 6161 is railcar W31W, which was providing the local service on the branch. The journey time was three minutes to Uxbridge and four to West Drayton. This is the southward view. (T.Wright)

XXI.   The station opened on 2nd October 1904, but housing development was still far from complete when this map was published in 1936.

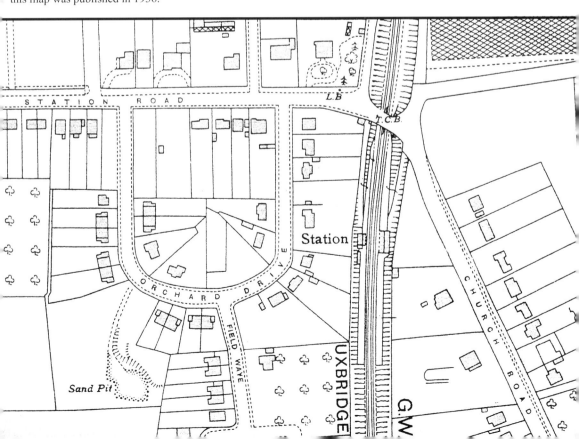

103.   We now have two pictures from 26th March 1962. By that time the service from Paddington was provided by DMUs of the type illustrated. The station had no signal box, but the Uxbridge distant can be seen beyond the bridge. (T.Wright)

104.   A train from Uxbridge passes under The Greenway and runs across land now occupied appropriately by Brunel University. The line was singled on 18th October 1962. The signal is the Uxbridge outer home. (T.Wright)

**UXBRIDGE
(VINE STREET)**

Church
Sun. Sch.

LYNCH Almshouses

B.M. 120·7

CHAPEL STREET

WINDSOR STREET

Grave Yard
(Disused)

P
P
P
P
P
P

Inn

VINE STREET

L.B.
W.M.

Goods Shed

Terminus

Vicarage

B.M. 116·4

School

110

B.M. 121·4

HINTON ROAD

MYDDLETON ROAD

107

C R O W

Town H.

C.C.D.

CRICKET FIELD ROAD

P

P

S.P.

S.B.

Cricket Ground

Pavilion

S.P.

XXII. The 1899 map shows the layout which changed little until another siding was laid behind the signal box in about 1924. Another followed in 1943. The engine shed is to the right of the main building. Locomotives had ceased to be kept there in 1897; the adjacent short siding had served a turntable.

104

I D G E

105. An overall roof was a feature of many early GWR stations; this was demolished in 1933, but an example can still be found at Frome. A Lancashire & Yorkshire wagon can be seen in the siding. The platform on the right was not signalled for arrivals. (LGRP/NRM)

106. The boarded platform would have given that now long-forgotten drumming sound under the heavy footware of the past, enhanced by the echo of the trainshed. The inverted seat suggests that dismantling is beginning. (British Rail)

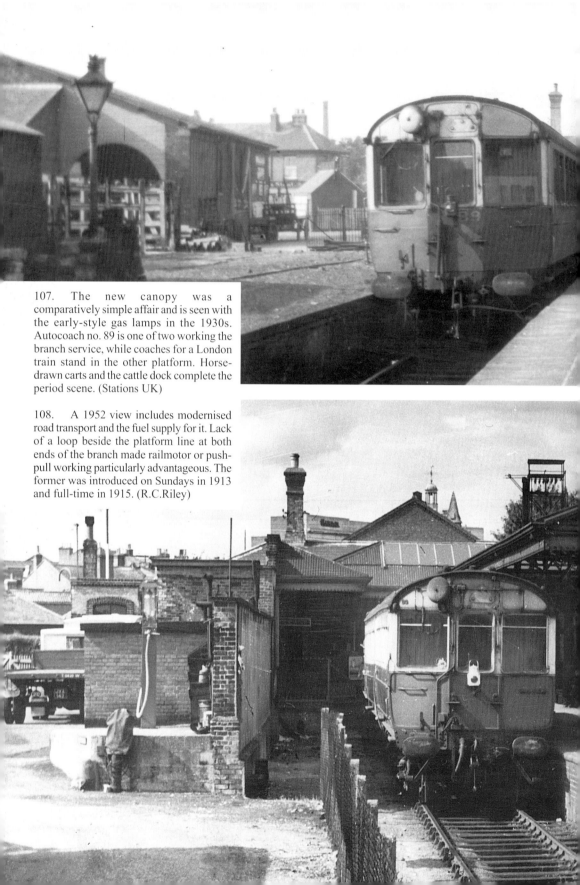

107. The new canopy was a comparatively simple affair and is seen with the early-style gas lamps in the 1930s. Autocoach no. 89 is one of two working the branch service, while coaches for a London train stand in the other platform. Horse-drawn carts and the cattle dock complete the period scene. (Stations UK)

108. A 1952 view includes modernised road transport and the fuel supply for it. Lack of a loop beside the platform line at both ends of the branch made railmotor or push-pull working particularly advantageous. The former was introduced on Sundays in 1913 and full-time in 1915. (R.C.Riley)

109. Railcars were even more economical when powered by diesel engines. The GWR were leaders in the application of such streamlined vehicles, the first appearing in 1934. No. W27W was recorded in July 1955, with tail lamp in place, ready to depart. (T.Wright)

110. The 2.20pm (Saturdays only) is being propelled into the platform after running round on 1st October 1955. It had previously worked down from Paddington. In the days of the 5½ day week, there was a rush hour in the middle of Saturdays. The 2-6-2T is no. 6169. (H.C.Casserley)

111. The van is unlikely to be connected to the train. One or more arrived early in the morning with "perishables", such as fruit, vegetables and fish. They usually remained there during the day. A large traffic in locally grown flowers was handled, many being destined for Birmingham. (Stations UK)

112.   With a tail lamp on the buffer beam, 0-4-2T no. 1462 is ready to return to West Drayton. The generously glazed roof had been a danger during wartime air raids, with the consequent shrapnel. (Lens of Sutton)

113.   Freight reached a peak in 1942, with a remarkable 107,514 tons being handled. Loading was facilitated by the 6-ton crane seen in this and the next picture. No. 8752 is departing on 20th May 1958. The siding in the foreground was added in about 1924 and was known as "Whitehall". (T.Wright)

114.   No. 1436 arrives with an autotrain on 27th September 1958, as no. 6128 waits to depart for Paddington. One electric light is evident, but the platform remained gaslit to the end, although electricity was used elsewhere from 1951. (A.E.Bennett)

115.   No. 6125 simmers at the buffer stops after arrival from London on 20th December 1958. Such trains called at all stations and took about 50 minutes, but steam traction ceased by the end of that month. The 6100 class had been introduced to the branch in 1931. (T.Wright)

116.   Passenger traffic was dwindling in 1962, such that a single railcar was sufficient on 26th March. However, freight traffic was still substantial. No. 9642 is busy while another locomotive blows off in the background. The goods yard closed on 13th July 1964. (T.Wright)

117.   By July 1965, the exterior was shabby compared with the nearby LT station. There had been an awning over the pavement until 1941, carrying GREAT WESTERN RAILWAY in one foot high letters. (T.Wright)

118. The 1920 signal box had 26 levers and was in use until 18th October 1962, when the branch was singled. The van is standing in "Manor Waye" siding in this September 1962 panorama. (J.C.Gillham)

119. With peak-hour operation only in the final four years, there was ample opportunity to examine the station uncluttered by trains. Part of the branch came back to life on 2nd July 1966, when the southern half-mile began to carry traffic to the Middlesex Oil & Chemical Works. However, this new siding closed on 8th January 1979. (J.C.Gillham)

120. The passenger entrance was closed for ever on 8th September 1962. Official closure was on the 10th. Soon the town would have only one instead of three stations and there would be only one instead of four branches of the Western Region in what is now the Greater London area. (T.Wright)

Middleton Press

Easebourne Lane, Midhurst, W Sussex. GU29 9AZ Tel: 01730 813169 Fax: 01730 812601
If books are not available from your local transport stockist, order direct with cheque,
Visa or Mastercard, post free UK.

BRANCH LINES
Branch Line to Allhallows
Branch Line to Alton
Branch Lines around Ascot
Branch Line to Ashburton
Branch Lines around Bodmin
Branch Line to Bude
Branch Lines around Canterbury
Branch Lines around Chard & Yeovil
Branch Lines around Cromer
Branch Lines to East Grinstead
Branch Lines of East London
Branch Lines to Effingham Junction
Branch Lines around Exmouth
Branch Line to Fairford
Branch Lines around Gosport
Branch Line to Hawkhurst
Branch Lines to Horsham
Branch Lines around Huntingdon
Branch Line to Ilfracombe
Branch Line to Kingswear
Branch Lines to Launceston & Princetown
Branch Lines to Longmoor
Branch Line to Looe
Branch Line to Lyme Regis
Branch Lines around March
Branch Lines around Midhurst
Branch Line to Minehead
Branch Line to Moretonhampstead
Branch Lines to Newport (IOW)
Branch Line to Padstow
Branch Lines around Plymouth
Branch Lines to Seaton and Sidmouth
Branch Line to Selsey
Branch Lines around Sheerness
Branch Line to Shrewsbury
Branch Line to Swanage *updated*
Branch Line to Tenterden
Branch Lines to Torrington
Branch Lines to Tunbridge Wells
Branch Line to Upwell
Branch Lines of West London
Branch Lines around Weymouth
Branch Lines around Wisbech

NARROW GAUGE BRANCH LINES
Branch Line to Lynton
Branch Lines around Portmadoc 1923-46
Branch Lines around Porthmadog 1954-94
Branch Line to Southwold
Kent Narrow Gauge
Two-Foot Gauge Survivors
Romneyrail
Southern France Narrow Gauge
Vivarais Narrow Gauge

SOUTH COAST RAILWAYS
Ashford to Dover
Bournemouth to Weymouth
Brighton to Eastbourne
Brighton to Worthing
Dover to Ramsgate
Eastbourne to Hastings
Hastings to Ashford
Portsmouth to Southampton
Southampton to Bournemouth

SOUTHERN MAIN LINES
Basingstoke to Salisbury
Bromley South to Rochester
Crawley to Littlehampton
Dartford to Sittingbourne
East Croydon to Three Bridges
Epsom to Horsham
Exeter to Barnstaple

Exeter to Tavistock
Faversham to Dover
London Bridge to East Croydon
Orpington to Tonbridge
Tonbridge to Hastings
Salisbury to Yeovil
Swanley to Ashford
Tavistock to Plymouth
Victoria to East Croydon
Waterloo to Windsor
Waterloo to Woking
Woking to Portsmouth
Woking to Southampton
Yeovil to Exeter

EASTERN MAIN LINES
Fenchurch Street to Barking
Ipswich to Saxmundham
Liverpool Street to Ilford

WESTERN MAIN LINES
Ealing to Slough
Exeter to Newton Abbot
Paddington to Ealing

COUNTRY RAILWAY ROUTES
Andover to Southampton
Bath Green Park to Bristol
Bath to Evercreech Junction
Bournemouth to Evercreech Jn.
Cheltenham to Andover
Croydon to East Grinstead
Didcot to Winchester
East Kent Light Railway
Fareham to Salisbury
Frome to Bristol
Guildford to Redhill
Porthmadog to Blaenau
Reading to Basingstoke
Reading to Guildford
Redhill to Ashford
Salisbury to Westbury
Stratford upon Avon to Cheltenham
Strood to Paddock Wood
Taunton to Barnstaple
Wenford Bridge to Fowey
Westbury to Bath
Woking to Alton
Yeovil to Dorchester

GREAT RAILWAY ERAS
Ashford from Steam to Eurostar
Clapham Junction 50 years of change
Festiniog in the Fifties
Festiniog in the Sixties
Isle of Wight Lines 50 years of change
Railways to Victory 1944-46
SECR Centenary album
Talyllyn 50 years of change
Yeovil 50 years of change

LONDON SUBURBAN RAILWAYS
Caterham and Tattenham Corner
Charing Cross to Dartford
Clapham Jn. to Beckenham Jn.
East London Line
Finsbury Park to Alexandra Palace
Kingston and Hounslow Loops
Lewisham to Dartford
Lines around Wimbledon
London Bridge to Addiscombe
Mitcham Junction Lines
North London Line
South London Line
West Croydon to Epsom
West London Line

Willesden Junction to Richmond
Wimbledon to Epsom

STEAMING THROUGH
Steaming through Cornwall
Steaming through Kent
Steaming through West Hants
Steaming through West Sussex

TRAMWAY CLASSICS
Aldgate & Stepney Tramways
Barnet & Finchley Tramways
Bath Tramways
Bournemouth & Poole Tramways
Brighton's Tramways
Burton & Ashby Tramways
Camberwell & W.Norwood Tramways
Clapham & Streatham Tramways
Croydon's Tramways
Dover's Tramways
East Ham & West Ham Tramways
Edgware and Willesden Tramways
Eltham & Woolwich Tramways
Embankment & Waterloo Tramways
Enfield & Wood Green Tramways
Exeter & Taunton Tramways
Greenwich & Dartford Tramways
Hammersmith & Hounslow Tramways
Hampstead & Highgate Tramways
Hastings Tramways
Holborn & Finsbury Tramways
Ilford & Barking Tramways
Kingston & Wimbledon Tramways
Lewisham & Catford Tramways
Liverpool Tramways 1. Eastern Routes
Liverpool Tramways 2. Southern Routes
Liverpool Tramways 3. Northern Routes
Maidstone & Chatham Tramways
North Kent Tramways
Norwich Tramways
Portsmouth's Tramways
Reading Tramways
Seaton & Eastbourne Tramways
Shepherds Bush & Uxbridge Tramways
Southampton Tramways
Southend-on-sea Tramways
Southwark & Deptford Tramways
Stamford Hill Tramways
Twickenham & Kingston Tramways
Victoria & Lambeth Tramways
Waltham Cross & Edmonton Tramways
Walthamstow & Leyton Tramways
Wandsworth & Battersea Tramways

TROLLEYBUS CLASSICS
Croydon Trolleybuses
Bournemouth Trolleybuses
Hastings Trolleybuses
Maidstone Trolleybuses
Reading Trolleybuses
Woolwich & Dartford Trolleybuses

WATERWAY ALBUMS
Kent and East Sussex Waterways
London to Portsmouth Waterway
West Sussex Waterways

MILITARY BOOKS
Battle over Portsmouth
Battle over Sussex 1940
Blitz over Sussex 1941-42
Bombers over Sussex 1943-45
Bognor at War
Military Defence of West Sussex
Secret Sussex Resistance
Sussex Home Guard

OTHER RAILWAY BOOKS
Garraway Father & Son
Index to all Middleton Press stations
Industrial Railways of the South-East
South Eastern & Chatham Railways
London Chatham & Dover Railway
War on the Line (SR 1939-45)